I0762651

Little Mitchie

RAINY DAY RECIPES

COZY FOOD FOR INDOOR FUN

KIDS IN THE KITCHEN

Joanne Mattern

CREATING YOUNG NONFICTION READERS

Little Mitchie books spark curiosity and support early nonfiction reading for students in Grades 2-3. Designed to build vocabulary, support second language learners, and prepare readers for middle-grade content, each book includes helpful tips for parents and educators to build confidence and deepen understanding of the world.

TIPS FOR READING NONFICTION WITH BEGINNING READERS

Talk about Nonfiction

Begin by explaining that nonfiction books give us information that is true. The book will be organized around a specific topic or idea, and we may learn new facts through reading.

Look at the Parts

Most nonfiction books have helpful features. Our *Little Mitchie* titles include color photographs and graphic aids, a table of contents, a glossary, and an index. Share the purpose of these features with your reader.

Color Photos and Graphic Aids

A lot of information can be found by "reading" photos, charts, maps, and other graphic aids found within nonfiction texts. Help your reader learn more about the different ways information can be displayed.

Table of Contents

Located at the front of the book, this list shows the big ideas within the text and the page numbers where they can be found.

Glossary

Located at the back of the book, the glossary defines key words and phrases that are related to the topic. These words and phrases can be found in the text in colored type.

Index

Located at the back of the book, an index is an alphabetical list of topics and the page numbers where they can be found.

With a little help and guidance about reading nonfiction, you can feel good about introducing a young reader to the world of *Little Mitchie* nonfiction books.

Little Mitchie is an imprint of:

PUBLISHERS

2001 SW 31st Avenue
Hallandale, FL 33009
mitchelllanepub.com

First Edition, 2027.

Author: Joanne Mattern
Designer: Bobbie Houser
Editor: Madison Greve

Library of Congress Cataloging-in-Publication Data
Title: Rainy Day Recipes: Cozy Food for Indoor Fun / by Joanne Mattern

Description: Hallandale, FL :
Mitchell Lane Publishers, [2027]

Identifiers:
ISBN 979-8-89260-930-2 (library bound)
ISBN 979-8-90145-016-1 (eBook)

Library of Congress Control Number: 2026936534

PHOTO CREDITS
Shutterstock: JeniFoto, cover, 1, 7; Taras Grebinets, 4; Viktoriia Ablohina, 5; Brent Hofacker, 9; Foodgraphy39, 11; Yaroshenko Maryna, 13; Dementieva Iryna, 15; Sohel_ctg, 17; iuliia_n, 19; PR Image Factory, 21.

TABLE OF

CONTENTS

HOW TO USE THIS BOOK

The kitchen is a great place to have fun! This book will help you make some delicious recipes.

Read each recipe first. Be sure to have everything you need in place before you start. Check that no one is **allergic** to any of the ingredients.

Wash your hands before you start.

Have an adult close by. Let them use knives and the stove.

Now, get ready to cook up some fun!

CONVERSION CHART

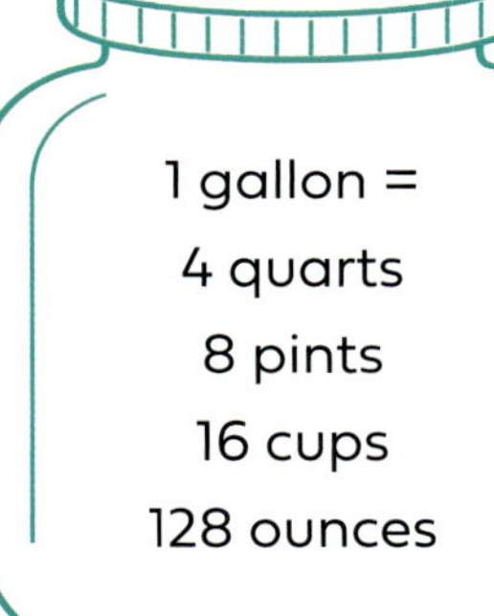

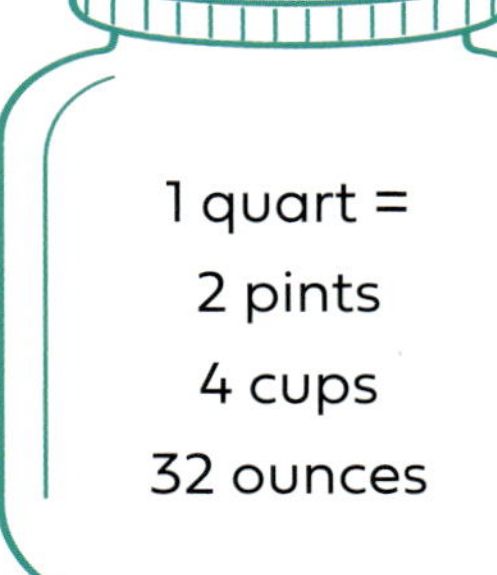

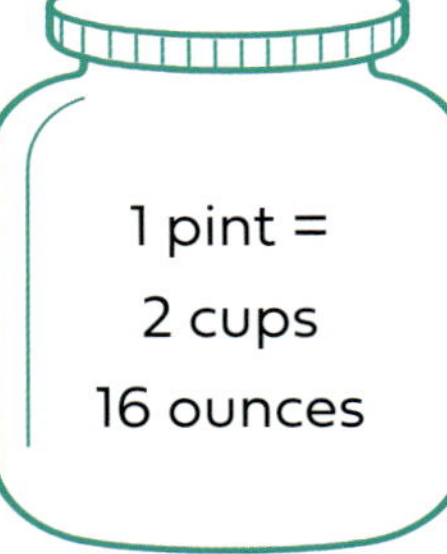

1 cup =	¾ cup =	½ cup =	⅓ cup =	¼ cup =
16 tablespoons	12 tablespoons	8 tablespoons	5 ⅓ tablespoons	4 tablespoons
8 ounces	6 ounces	4 ounces	2 ⅔ ounces	2 ounces

3 teaspoons = 1 tablespoon (½ ounce)
2 tablespoons = ⅛ cup (1 ounce)
4 tablespoons = ¼ cup (2 ounces)
5 ⅓ tablespoons = ⅓ cup (2 ⅔ ounces)
8 tablespoons = ½ cup (4 ounces)
12 tablespoons = ¾ cup (6 ounces)
32 tablespoons = 2 cups (16 ounces)

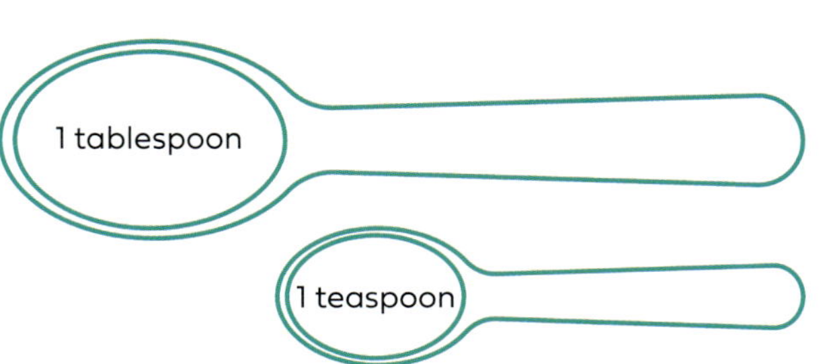

Chapter 1

FROZEN BANANA POPS

"What a soaking-wet morning!" Peter exclaimed. He sat down at the table. "I guess I will be staying inside today. But I would like something fun for breakfast."

"Here is a recipe you might like," his mother said. "You love bananas and yogurt. Let's **combine** them and make a colorful breakfast! That will brighten up a gloomy day."

Peter looked at the recipe.
“What a fun idea!” he said.
“I’ll get the ingredients ready.”

You will need:

4 bananas

¾-cup strawberry or vanilla yogurt

8 Popsicle™ sticks

3–4 different toppings (¾-cup each)

Directions:

Scoop the yogurt into a bowl and cover a baking sheet with wax paper.

Pour the toppings onto different plates. Use small toppings like cereal or sprinkles.

Peel each banana. Then ask an adult to cut each banana in half through the middle, not from top to bottom.

With the pointed end of the banana facing up, stick a Popsicle™ stick through the middle bottom of each banana half. Make sure you can hold them like lollipops.

Dip a banana in the yogurt and make sure it is covered all the way around. Then roll the banana in a plate of your toppings and place on the wax paper.

When all of the bananas are covered, place the baking sheet in the freezer for about 1 hour.

FUN FOOD FACT!
The pieces of cereal in a box of Froot Loops™ come in different colors, but each color is the same **flavor**.

Chapter 2

SWEET POPCORN TREAT

Finn looked at the rain pouring down outside. “Today is a good day to stay in and watch a movie,” he said to his brother, Alex.

“Great idea! Let’s make some popcorn to eat while we watch,” Alex said. “Remember the sweet popcorn we had at that party? Let’s ask Dad if we can make it ourselves.”

Finn and Alex told their father about their idea. "We can do that," Dad said. "You make the **seasoning** and I'll make the popcorn. Then we'll all watch the movie together."

You will need:

½-cup popcorn kernels

8 tablespoons brown sugar

1½ teaspoons salt

4 teaspoons ground cinnamon

1 teaspoon olive oil

3 tablespoons unsalted butter

Directions:

Mix the sugar, cinnamon, and salt in a cup to make the seasoning.

Ask an adult to make the popcorn. Pour the olive oil into a pan and add the kernels when the oil is hot. Carefully cover the pan with a lid and wait for the kernels to pop!

Ask an adult to melt the butter on the stove or in the microwave.

With an adult's help, pour the melted butter over the popcorn.

Shake the seasoning over the popcorn. Mix well.

FUN FOOD FACT!
Scientists discovered popcorn kernels in a cave in New Mexico. They were over 5,600 years old!

Chapter 3

GOOEY GRILLED CHEESE

"It's such a cold, wet day," Alice complained to her aunt. "Can we have something warm for lunch?"

"Of course," Aunt Pat said. "I know just the thing. There is nothing better than a grilled cheese sandwich. Do you want to help me?"

"I'd love to!" Alice replied. "Let's use lots of cheese to make it extra gooey!"

"Great idea!" Aunt Pat said. She took out the frying pan. "Let's get started."

You will need:

2 slices of white bread

4 thin slices of cheese (cheddar, mozzarella, or Colby-Jack are good choices)

Butter

Directions:

Place 1 slice of bread on a plate and cover with a few slices of cheese.

Place the other slice of bread on top.

Spread a thin layer of butter on the top slice.

Ask an adult to melt butter in a small frying pan.

Ask an adult to place the unbuttered side of the sandwich into the melted butter.

Cook for approximately 3 minutes, until the bread is golden-brown.

Ask an adult to flip the sandwich over. Cook for another few minutes.

Use a **spatula** to move the sandwich onto a plate.

FUN FOOD FACT!
Grilled cheese sandwiches used to be called toasted cheese or melted cheese sandwiches.

Chapter 4

NO-BAKE COOKIE DELIGHTS

Theresa was bored. She and her sister were stuck inside on a rainy day.

"We need to have some fun," said her older sister, Margaret. "Let's make some cookies!"

"We're not allowed to use the oven," Theresa said.

"We don't need to for these cookies," Margaret said. "No baking required! And it's okay for me to use the stovetop."

Theresa was curious. She followed Margaret into the kitchen. How can you make cookies without baking them? She was about to find out!

You will need:

2 cups sugar

¼-cup unsweetened cocoa powder

½-cup milk

½-cup butter

1 teaspoon vanilla extract

1 pinch salt

3 cups minute oats

½-cup peanut butter

ALLERGY ALERT!

Directions:

Mix the milk, butter, sugar, and cocoa in a **saucepan**. Ask an adult to boil the mixture for approximately 90 seconds.

With an adult's help, stir in the peanut butter, vanilla, and oats.

Use a spoon to scoop the mixture onto the wax paper. Be careful! The mixture will be very hot.

Flatten each cookie with a spoon.

Place the tray in the refrigerator until the cookies harden.

GLOSSARY

allergic (uh-LER-jik)—having a bad reaction to a food

combine (kum-BINE)—mix together

flavor (FLAY-vor)—the way something tastes

saucepan (SAWSS-pan)—a small, deep pot

seasoning (SEEZ-uh-ning)—ingredients that make food taste more interesting

spatula (SPAT-yoo-lah)—a kitchen tool with a long handle and a flat blade that is used for flipping or lifting

FURTHER READING

McEvedy, Allegra. *Chefs Wanted: More Than 40 Delicious Recipes for Curious Cooks.* Dorling Kindersley, 2024.

Saltz, Joanna. *The How-To Cookbook for Young Foodies.* Hearst Home Kids, 2025.

ON THE INTERNET

Barclay, Lily. "Rainy Day Cooking Projects for Kids." Good Food.com
https://www.bbcgoodfood.com/howto/guide/rainy-day-cooking-projects-kids
This article includes recipes for clever and fun meals, snacks, and desserts.

Bull, Marian. "7 Kid-Friendly Cooking Projects for a Rainy Day." Food52.com.
https://food52.com/story/4796-7-kid-friendly-cooking-projects-for-a-rainy-day
This article has many different recipes for kids and adults to make and bake together.

INDEX

ABOUT THE AUTHOR

Joanne Mattern loves snacking and eating fun food! She has written many nonfiction books for children, including cookbooks and books about holidays. Joanne lives in New York State with her family.